*Designed to Fade*

# Mary Coghill

## *Designed to Fade*

Shearsman Books
Exeter

Published in the United Kingdom in 2006 by
Shearsman Books Ltd
58 Velwell Road
Exeter EX4 4LD

ISBN-13    978-1-905700-05-9

ISBN-10    1-905700-05-9

Copyright © Mary Coghill, 2006.

The right of Mary Coghill to be identified as the author of this work has been asserted by her in accordance with the Copyrights, Designs and Patents Act of 1988. All rights reserved. No part of this publication may be reproduced, stored in a retrieval system, transmitted in any form or by any means, electronic, mechanical, photocopying, recording or otherwise, without the prior permission of the publisher.

Cover: 'Tram Stop – Streetwise series', © 2002 Désirée Palmen
www.desireepalmen.nl
Courtesy Reuten Galerie, Amsterdam.

## Acknowledgements

I would like to acknowledge the expert assistance of the Women's Library at London Metropolitan University and also the Library at Sussex University, which houses the Leonard Woolf Collection. I am grateful to Tony Lopez, Professor in Poetry at the University of Plymouth, for his excellent and consistently helpful advice. I also thank Mary Jacobs for her valuable assistance. Any shortcomings or errors in this poem are mine.

My thanks go also to The Ronald Duncan Foundation whose generous financial support enabled me to undertake the MA dissertation for which this poem was written, and to the University of Plymouth Press for their expressions of confidence and assistance in the early stages of this publication. Joseph Brown helped with the the design of this book, and I am grateful for his assistance.

My personal thanks go to Sheila and Sandra.

This publication has been funded by a generous grant from
Arts Council England (London).

# CONTENTS

| | |
|---|---|
| Dedication | 9 |
| Prologue | 11 |
| Foundation Poem | 13 |
|     *Kaleidoscopically* | 16 |
| Night into Day | 19 |
|     *She Died in Her Bed This Night* | 20 |
|     *Manhunt* | 21 |
|     *The Prince and his Mistress* | 23 |
| Get Up | 25 |
|     *Ode to the City* | 29 |
|     *way* | 32 |
|     *I/You* | 33 |
| Reading on the Tube | 35 |
| Arrival at Work | 39 |
|     *Facts* | 42 |
|     *But There's No Need to Laugh at Her* | 43 |
|     *And Nemesis?* | 44 |
| All in a Day's . . . | 47 |
|     *Irony* | 48 |
|     *Morning Meeting* | 52 |
|     *The City is Body* | 54 |
|     *The City as Simile* | 55 |
|     *The City is Metaphor* | 56 |
| Impetus and Structure for Lunch | 59 |
|     *Metonymy has the Property of Contiguity* | 60 |
|     *Metonymy and Emotion* | 61 |
|     *Designed to Fade* | 64 |
|     *City Crane* | 65 |
|     *Ashes* | 68 |
|     *Annual Lunch* | 70 |
| Afternoon | 73 |
|     *Ideogrammatical Taxonomic Urbis* | 74 |
|     *City Exam* | 76 |
|     *A Manifesto: OED NW1* | 78 |

| | |
|---|---:|
| Parks | 83 |
| *The Unreliable Narrator* | 85 |
| *Elegy by Images to the Passing of Words* | 87 |
| Going Home/Kinetics | 89 |
| *Rush Hour* | 92 |
| *A Wilderness Metaphor* | 94 |
| *Fractally* | 95 |
| Symposium | 103 |
| *Women Unite Reclaim the Night* | 109 |
| Lullaby | 111 |
| | |
| Afterword | 114 |
| Biographical Notes | 115 |
| Notes | 116 |

# Designed to Fade

— *A Narrative Poem* —

# Dedication

lettertounknownfriend@citylocation.org

Dear unknown friend
        Survivor in arms
        can you spare the time
        to recognise whether the writer has understood
I have known you exist for many years

I have loved this city
        still love this city
measure my years of growth
        seize my catalogue of achievements
            by this city
        extend my hopes for this city that
        'When one fled past . . . her name was Hope'

would it be enough to say I hear voices
        study heteroglossia
            in the interests of racial harmony
        wander the streets of SE5/N21
        find the kernel of ideas
        say which day it is
            the picture is overall or regional
        see headlines:
                . . . walker expresses concern for city streets
                'no go' hits city junction
                'not enough' for walk out nurses
                Straw catches mood of epidemic

I have understood that poetic forces may be at work
        are there devices here?
            we are together on this one
            we have walked these streets
            been through gates
            walked up steps
            opened doors
                is it the precise location you are after?
                The Grove The Warren
                      Copse Drive

    warning
        there is a moment's stasis
                my privacy
      I have lived in this city
          continue to live in it
once when I woke
I heard the roar of traffic on Hanger Lane
    I have never forgotten it
      planes thunder or purr overhead
I retread familiar streets to everyday destinations
    those days when I don't go
    the days when I would not go
we all of us dream of the place beyond

# Prologue

Dear Reader
    grown      from request
    sought      by need
    created      by a woman's words
    clarified      by energy
    thinking      I could do you a service
    I have spoken      to the night and day
         to the critics and lovers
         the supervisors and friends
    consulted      my almanac
         then
    take      out the personal
    metonymise      emotions
    attend      to the chaotic
    produce      a semblance of objectified energy
    put in      some focus
    construct      a prosodic technique
    devise      the narrative
    understand      alienation and mimesis
    achieve      equivalence
growing up positions
chart this labyrinthine map which
on account of its lack of compass markings
is impossible to read
set the mechanism in motion
it will start anywhere go anywhere
our destinations are unknown
now
all along the corridors and up and down the stairs
with only a ball of string
tied to the first memory
then on to other memories
it runs out it runs out
gyroscopic stability mocking stasis
the unknown the not understood
leaving us only today and tomorrow

## Foundation Poem

List the founding fathers and mothers
extoll the founding virtues and errors
inspire the founding energies and frustrations
        count yourself lucky

This is a great city   A-Z
encompassed by literal measurements
        OS grid references
                heights and depths
we think of the underground and the overground
we read about the mains cables
        sewers telephone wires
            the flight paths
                the neck aching upward vistas
                      the sodium and halogen auras

      there are layers of
              dialogic heterodoxy
              dreadful night  awful day
              one or many
              organisation  chaos
      the city of constantly renewing our bargain
                  of never being the same
                  of always being there
                  exploration not explication


Great City built on hope  effort  greed  communication
Great City built with bricks  glass  cement  steel
Great City built on water  land  marsh  downs
Great City built with hard work  energy  ideas  passion
Great City built on poverty  degradation  criminality  forces
      Settle neatly under the stars
            that outlive you
      Rise up each morning
      Shake yourself in the steam that rises with the sun
            that outlives you
      March earnestly through the day creating more heat more dust

                    with the air that outlasts you
Slow down in the evenings
            with pregnant echoes that resound
            memories that you will not recall

## *Kaleidoscopically*

here are invariably housing
and Giant Gherkin with inside lit light
twist watch mosaics fall into place
histo-sorrowfully backward vistas
trailing lights against tumbling colour
back lit beautifully through windows
irrevocably greys blues and browns
alternatively aspirations
rejects venously the forms shake out
into place form dash through ugliness
interchangeably piecemeal and fall
diffusely riotously into
let's and out of here and there quickly
transiently of pockets I want
shall necessarily poverty
restlessly through Maida Vale Hackney
capriciously sorted through by chance
located centrifugally thrown
suburban surround delightfully
it's the dusty dramatic of it
windswept in echo of romantic
wistfully no yes once unwanted
moment's poise delightfully children
say we are happy all perspective
alters by fragment by moment by
dome or line or link unlock we think
science places inconstantly whilst
reflectively degradation holds
there are whilst travelling hopefully
on the rustling cascade of fragments
music of the earthly spheres these are
these are the people thankfully yours
respectfully to inspectors who
just asking for money whilst busking
managerially we need a
shake up if I can only get a
taxi first left south of the river
pointing sunward blinding quicksilver

do I love you relentlessly still
movingly hateful pieces tumble
to the rim stickily come to visit
annoyingly the pattern repeats
this requires attention it doesn't need
this turning fast powerfully held
to ransom traffic warden plumber
phone phone you must come to the phone in
dependently we hold hands he needs
help manifestly reversibly
humanly I am yours tickets guard
caretaker take mine when thrown away
carelessly poets calling pieces
use notes from page to sound from pattern
to falling to change all change lovers
                                              then and now

# Night into Day

## She Died in Her Bed This Night

    I hear her **screaming**
    I hear her **screaming**
      and when it **stops**
          I hear his feet **running**
    it's the sound of his feet **running**
          I can hear **running**
  the sound of feet running down the **stairs**
                it's my **mother**
    I hear the thud as she falls to the **floor**
                  my mouth is **dry**
      I hear feet running all the way down **stairs**
        I hear the thud of the front door **shut**
                  I hear **screaming**
  it's the screaming it doesn't stop I hear him **swearing**
                I hear him **shouting**
I hear her **screaming**      and when the screaming **stops**
  and when it **stops**    I hear my heart thudding **thudding**
      I hear his feet **running**    heartbeat ringing in my **ears**
it's the sound of his feet **running**
      I can hear **running**
the sound of feet running down the **stairs**
            it's my **mother**
  I hear the thud as she falls to the **floor**
              my mouth is **dry**
    I hear feet running all the way down **stairs**
      I hear the thud of the front door **shut**
              I hear **screaming**
  it's the screaming it doesn't stop I hear him **swearing**
              I hear him **shouting**
          and when the screaming **stops**
       I hear my heart thudding **thudding**
          heartbeat ringing in my **ears**

## *Manhunt*

fierce hot summer's night
where darkness hardly closes in
coolness is barely remembered
covers are thrown back
sweat recoats sensate pallid skin
stir grasp a thin breath of moving
air by the open window turn
pillow over draw curtains back
stare at hostile light splenetic sky
battered by dust sounds of traffic
tube trains rattling to a depot
auras of foetid tunnel heat
traffic roars and nearby seems
peaceful near distant shouts laughter
the pub shuts footsteps ring languid
from the street below I sigh
turn onto my back so hot so
hot so hot I must have dozed
half hearing the people downstairs
their front door closes half silence
in full heat light sleep in heavy
close darkness suddenly
sounds spell disaster
I am wide awake here
near the house under the window
small rustlings from many sources
furtive rapid shuffling urgent
someone's out of breath
I lean over the cill look out
I can see nothing lit by
orange eyes of Cerberus' gleam
then louder more urgent footsteps
scuffling muffled imprecation
I hear the cries of the hunters
the police it's the police where?
what? I hear several I sense
he moved I can see nothing
but they are nearer

the bushes in a front garden
pushed aside trodden on soft cries
here no try here no he's not here look
sibilant whispers urgent break
muscular power drives their sound
focus fierce determination
quiet deliberate hush
Then a blood up yell of cheerful
triumph got him he's here! here!
piercing animal shriek trapped man
I see no bushes swaying snapping
cluster of struggling arms and legs
he's gone quietly now shadows loom
they lead him round the corner
a van door opens clang metal
slams metal a sickening thud
unique sound of human skull
bone hitting metal at speed
'you're nicked' I can see nothing
when the van has driven away
the low whispers between others cease
I lay back onto the bare sheet
it's now 3.00 o'clock I do not sleep

## *The Prince and his Mistress*

'At a blow I have lost my health
and nearly my daughter as well,
In the present I mourn past loss
through life of deepening shadow.

'I remember our passion, sweet
waves breaking over and over,
loving, caressing tired cheeks
our elixir wordless at one.

'Faltering to me in darkness
reluctant yet ruling my heart,
yours, uncertainty and longing –
I simply became your mistress.

'Then, after year long innocence
I knew I was nothing to you,
knowledge, ending ignorance, light
revealing it seems, only seems.

'Your face held sweet pain of decay,
first love beckoned, commanded,
taunted, overrode you, needed you,
compulsive fulsome alliance.

'Your looks, mixing fear and hope –
amidst desire, love making –
change – nervous, distant, aloof,
and morning sets all to naught.

'You knew that your first love held you,
how hell fills the night without her,
how dawn makes escape impossible,
how, oh how, she entices, traps, rules.

'As your mistress, greatly loving,
I was the innocent, untried,
I who came second, now set free,
she who came first, has you in chains.

'Mocking white serpentine Queen,
mistress of passion's parody,
banishes you where shadows reign;
crack wrecked in curling throes.'

# Get Up

Wrench corporeality out of bed
solidify dreams to naught
conquer blurs in indoor bathroom light
        I can settle all problems by watchfulness
        I mourned seriously the loss of night
        oh I look dreadful in this mirror
        the Sphinx arrives: AAHHH
*'I wake from daydreams to this real night'*
*'the sworded angel's wrecks, the sphinx supreme'*
you think you may be my witness
        (author's footnote to the poet:
                you lack the qualities of terminal illness or
                drugged despair)
so you think this is significant?
        Sphinx: HUH
she *'who represents perhaps things-as-they-are;*
        *the Truth'*
        Sphinx: HMMM
will you
tramp the streets
                of the city
visit the homes
                of the city
call in at the offices
                of the city
duck and dodge
                around the wards of the city's hospitals
                the cells of police stations
are you tempted
to drop in on
                wily politicians who will say
                'you will be regulated by new laws'

Dear Sphinx
I must eat breakfast
I can tell by your lack of response
this is not what you are looking for
Dear Sphinx do you require obeisance?

        supplications? prayers?
shocked recognition of your
        power        self-control
        intelligence        reason
        dedication        persistence
        calmness        passion
        manifestations of fallibility
            through our reflections
        you are hot        uncuddly
        forbidding        mysterious
        quiescent        statuesque
                please may I just
                go about the business
                of waking up to another
                day?
    Sphinx: MMMHUH
I HAVE brought you a song
as one last offering
    *'I wake from nightmares to this real day'*

From begging for my life
to a man who holds a knife
and demands gratuitous death,
*'I wake from nightmares to this real day'*

From struggling with lock, guile
of one who entraps with wiles,
with human hope's sweet Judas kiss,
*'I wake from nightmares to this real day'*

From half-felt passing hours
stiff joints from work, dreams, powers
shattered by alarm – seven,
*'I wake from nightmares to this real day'*

From fear, repeated blows,
learnt memories in fibrous
muscle, tensile repetitions,
*'I wake from nightmares to this real day'*

From someone who torments
in dreams long after, re-taunts

from trauma, left long behind me
*'I wake from nightmares to this real day'*

From concentrated voices
those who want what's mine, forces
push me, running till sky is stone
*'I wake from nightmares to this real day'*

## Ode to the City

City　City　City
head　heart　body　soul
I reason with the city
    collate
      collect
        sift
rescind
start out and try again
    false starts as part of the future pattern
where would I be without the crescendo of voices
    the roar of buses
    lorries accelerating
    over the manhole that has clanked unlevel for years
the glancing flashes of the tubes
    cradle rocked lopsided glow-worms
    burrowing out of the breaking dawn
that nothing ever happens exactly the same
    7.00am a chill dim dawn
    years passing
astonishment at meeting people by chance
    'I went into the army and left after a day'
    'I'm up for attempted murder I always did have a temper'
a sweat of fear
    when the drug dealer bouncer moved in next door
    sit behind a security door
    listen to the junkies whooping
      crying out all along the corridors
    or sit in safety and look at Crimewatch
there are varying degrees of hope and quietude
    various strengths of bravery in adversity
    to recognise the known is not an asset for the future
person to person
    I smile at the woman next to me in the Breast clinic
    we are reassured together
there is a life to be lived amongst total strangers
    amongst people we hardly
    or indeed do not want to know
we are precise and delicate at avoiding physical contact

                        careful in talking in voices that do not carry
we tightly hold plastic bags
            children
            so that nothing gets trampled on
            swept unwittingly away
we are on guard
            against predators
            looking for one who is separated from the crowd
                        those who carry a map but can no longer use it
                                    cry for help and it does not come
                                    hold out for a lifeline in the city
                        when there is nothing between them
                        and the stars
                                    sickening terrors in the night
            those who are sensitised to noise
            hear hell opening its jaws
                        when all we want to do is sleep

a poem of beauty
            will miss the tone of the huge unfolding city mass
a single story
            will be parochial
archives Acts and Commissions
            will gloss over daily life
desire for money
            will omit all who live with major fear or trauma
repetition brings ease of mind
the aspiration is to carry on the same?
we may reserve formality for unfamiliar occasions
      satirise abusively
            the politician who is blindly humiliated
         join a pressure group
                  be measured and just in our deductions
            love our children dearly
                  get angry when we fight for their good
we have all of these voices and more
      I am artful about them up to a point
      they are all a part of me
                  as city
         the poet as city conscious of
                  which voice as city

which part of self as city
crisscrossing the various pathways
roads   routes   streets
events
           time passing
                     binding us

## *way*

memory obliterates colours – cars
except – precise time of day
way to work – early
I have crossed – will cross
day after day – day after day

        the cars – specific road
        precision – a day when
        about the slab – this road
        cold air – look up
        ready and amber – ready and amber

cross now – driver who might
stop – misunderstanding
not know – too late to know
coincidence – stopped
coincides – coincides

        Goldhawk Road – if there had been any
        last time – moment of reflection
        eyes – but not misunderstanding
        last moments – moving cars
        not too late – not too late

coincidence – each other's eyes
move – reflections
precise colour – morning crossing
cold air – just this once
stops then – stops then

        time of day – pulling away
        eyes crossing – morning colour
        numbers – specific memory
        8.08 – irritation 8.08
        Chiswick High Road – Chiswick High Road

## *I/You*

You are not at all sure that complaining about the lorries late at night is the right thing to do. You know this is a residential area and that they shouldn't be roaring though at 2.30am, but the time it takes to find the right number, the right department, be put off by people who are so much more relaxed than you and who have so much more time than you – well put it in writing – no I'm not paid to write letters, you are paid to enforce the regulations and I'm asking you to do it. You are not sure you will have these reserves of sharpness today – but later – the Symposium – 'oh that's something I would much rather go to.'

In the bitter early morning when you left the hospital at least the bus is warm. Warmth is something you left behind when he left you. You wish that the bus ride would last for hours, that there would be no more decisions to make. You wish that the last 2 days was never, that your life could be changed by turning a knob and making a different selection, 'but this is no longer my home'. What are you going to do? You will make tea, go to bed. You do not know if there is anything in the house to eat. You do not wish to recall all the recent details. You are turning away your head when you speak to me, you are becoming more distant. I would really like to know, but you are adamant. You have a meeting to go to 'would you like to come?' You half smile, you only ever wanted kindness but you chose the wrong lover, now you must begin all over again. 'I will not tell your secrets,' I say. You are packing your self away again. I've pushed it and your London stockade is going up around you. Rock and a hard place, you're on the road packed and ready to go.

# Reading on the Tube

Plato
Dear Plato
O Great Plato
Great Greek disciple of great ancient democracy
how glad I am you mentioned women a few times in your Republic
we are pleased to be here
to be recognised as having some function in your great plan of things
mind you I notice that you rather skate off in another direction
in a not too organised manner
which means you just lost interest after a few pages
how wonderful that you found so many other things more important
how glad I am to take this opportunity to undertake a life
according to your dictates
well now let me see

*"'. . . and on the women (rulers – this word is left out of the main text and relegated to a footnote) too, Glaucon," said I; "for you must not suppose that my words apply to the men more than to all women who arise among them endowed with the requisite qualities.'"*

women – we emerge in all our glory in Book 5

*"'For we have long been lying in wait for you, expecting that you would say something both of the procreation of children and their bringing up, and would explain the whole matter of the community of women and children . . .'"*

*"'What a thing you have done," said I, "in thus challenging me! What a huge debate you have started afresh . . .'"*

*"'Nay Socrates," said Glaucon . . . "the measure of listening to such discussions is the whole of life for reasonable men. So don't consider us, and do not you yourself grow weary in explaining to us what we ask for, your views as to how this communion of wives and children among our guardians will be managed . . .'"*

*"'It is not an easy thing to expound, my dear fellow . . . For which reason one, as it were, shrinks from touching on the matter lest the theory be regarded as nothing but a 'wish-thought' . . .'"*

how you then dive into doubts and procrastinations
so we are too difficult to deal with
merely a 'wish-thought'
we raise your hackles Socrates and I'm glad

      Sphinx hey Sphinx look what I've found tucked away here
          a wish-thought or two
        called women and children (the education of)
         who are you having a dialogue with
          not me (I think the Sphinx said that)
           Socrates has interrupted
           listen to his pseudo humility

*"'My good fellow, is that remark intended to encourage me?" "It is," he said. "Well then," said I, "it has just the contrary effect . . . But to speak when one doubts himself and is seeking while he talks, as I am doing, is a fearful and slippery venture. The fear is not of being laughed at, for that is childish . . .""*

         well I agree with you here Socrates
      but I wasn't there and you weren't speaking to me
       (imagine if I were speaking these words)
    did you ask me a question about women and our status in society
   'well to speak when I doubt myself and am seeking while I talk
           as I am doing
        is a slippery and exciting venture'
           ha got you
         you put in different words
       you're not even starting from the same position
        the Sphinx has definitely arrived

*"'For, indeed, I believe that involuntary homicide is a lesser fault than to mislead opinion about the honourable, the good, and the just.'"*

         They are getting stuck in now
         covering their positions
   in case someone says they are not talking about the right things
        I have covered all my positions
      in case I am told I am writing all about the wrong things

*"'then the laughter of the eyes faded away before that which reason revealed to be best . . .'"*

        If only I could place my faith in reason
        when so many place theirs in God
         or unquestioned privilege
      accepting as of right that which they have
      I glance between Socrates and the Sphinx
          are they enemies?
         well known to each other?
     he looks as if he's about to ask THAT question

                    the Sphinx shifts in a leisurely way
                                              and
                                    taking her time
          she flexes her wings before speaking
                there is nothing more enraging
                      nothing more engaging
                            than others' errors
                                  I get mad
                                              I get mad
                                              at an expression of culture that contains
                                              no effort at technique
                                              it is not enough just to state
                                              record fact and ask us to ponder a truth
                                              to present fact as culture without art
                                              is therefore the recording of tragedy
                                              as culture without art an act of
                                              pornography?
                                  this is some Alienation Effect

**Arrival at Work**

stride purposefully up the steps
        what will you do now?
        the horrors   the difficulties
        the powerlessness   the brutality is there
        where will you go?
        be a refugee from your own city?
push through the automatic doors to work
        you can say to yourself well I work for the money
        I work hard
        the labourer is worthy of his (sic) hire
smile at Mary the receptionist
        Madam said Plato with an attempt at deference
        I defy you to laugh she said
        will you just take the facts and present them
take the lift or the stairs?
        woman gives birth man kills baby woman tells police?
        where is the culture here?
        In our republic began Plato
lift doors open
        I think I saw the Sphinx ruffle her feathers but I'm not sure
        would she really demonstrate contempt?
        No irony – got it
        No facts
nod to someone in lift I don't like
        only fun, fantasy, pleasure and pain
        we are not sure who said this
        Socrates was rock still
        Plato wasn't very vocal
yes seventh floor for me
        you are confusing things
        it really is all quite clear said the Sphinx
        things are always clear to those who carry a lot of weight
        said Plato under his breath
        I could so easily have sniggered
        but felt the laughter fade
manager gets in on fourth floor
        do I have to take these things seriously
        yes said the Sphinx

        how on earth can we construct stories
        artfully with tragedy or comedy
        without any basis in fact whatsoever
        yes said Plato yes indeed how
        we must be able to recognise what is being portrayed
let manager get out first
        something that bears no resemblance
        will not be recognised
        cannot be recognised by us
        we can make no comparison
        we can certainly take facts, the Sphinx went on
        and comment on them without irony even comically
        but without irony
        the irony is a refusal to be there with the story
        absorbed in the events that are being unfolded before us
security code doesn't work
they've changed it AGAIN
        'I'm sure I've been through this before,' I snapped
        no you haven't said the Sphinx
        without question this is a first
manager lets me through with a sneer

## *Facts*

I have opened my mail and
I record the ensuing facts
    I got up from a clean and comfortable bed
    one winter's morning and turned on the tap
    washed in hot water
    and ate a breakfast of my choice before going to work
        I did not get up in a damp room
        with only dirty clothes to put on
        and go to work without breakfast
        and without washing because there was no hot water
you will point the finger at me and say this was my choice
I hold up the energy bills
    point at the totals
    and state that I am only earning the minimum wage
the laughter fades
the art fades the culture fades
the irony and playfulness are quite abandoned
    but may we not warm the chill page with an ornament of generosity
        here you've dropped your ticket
    a curlicue of a pun
        did you catch the bus this morning – no it went faster than me
   a twist of empathy
       are you sure you're alright dear?

            well eventually we all got to the bit
        where the old women have taken off all their clothes
          and are practicing in the gymnasium
       whilst the men are suppressing improper derision
     well you may have plucked the unripe fruit of laughter

## But There's No Need to Laugh at Her

two policemen drive a hard bargain with dignity
they pick her up off the concrete path and dump her back on the seat
all in tatters and dirt she falls sideways and rolls to the back of the bench
they laugh

look at her filthy scum she'll fall off again in a minute
and that's just what she did talking all the time a world of nonsense
mumbling drunken purposeless movements twitching
they laugh

I walk over to them  excuse me what is the matter
why don't you help that woman up  they sneer
she doesn't need help  take her to hospital she'll only walk out
they laugh

one of them sits her up and she slumps again
face down on the bench shipwrecked jetsam in sunlit park
London morning living all around her taking no notice
do not laugh at her

I think of some of my past expensive mistakes
a woman trying to entice me into prostitution
a man who said he loved me tricking me with drugs
do not laugh at me

triumphant with bedsit independence a job that drove me
to drink  tears shed after laughter  hopes punch drunk
love ricocheting down the cracks in a golden pavement
do not laugh at me

## And Nemesis?

such an ally in a roughcast world
valiant with bags and determined plotting
the route to the convent for breakfast
then back again shouting vigorously
hectoring the world without a parliament
carrying her baggage of spare clothes and vitriol
stopping at moments of intensity
putting down her bags and really letting rip
*'but in these very duties lighter tasks must be assigned to the women than to the men because of their weakness as a class'*
right across the busy road I could hear the sounds of explosive words
the builders in the house next door took her on
eff off you old bag they shouted
she rolled by with heavy laden gait
eff off you old cow
with that she turned and let fly
get lost you effing effers
the vicious energetic fountain of obscenities
rolled forcefully over the tops of cars
under the chasses of lorries
the builders gathered – all five of them
waving fists you old effing c clear off you c you daft c yerr
and they laughed at her
she never wavered and her voice never broke
the bags remained where they were
      on the pavement
           and her voice carried
                and carried
                    and carried
looking over at the builders
I saw them turn tail and go inside the house
and shut the door
      shut the door
           now she was left alone
she picked up her bags and ambled away
When I saw her next I gave her money
every time after that she shouted at me
there's a lovely lady there's a fine friend

then I realised I hadn't seen her for a long time
memory doesn't always fade
cursing isn't a job I would give a man
they're just not strong enough
to clear the streets

**All in a Day's . . .**

## *Irony*

    Meeting of Minds: 11 a.m.
    Minutes of the last meeting dated 21st: Read and Signed
    Chair: Reader
    Those present: Poet Author Memory Narrator Witness
                Unknown Friend
    Apologies for Absence: Reason
    Agenda: Irony

| | |
|---|---|
| Narrator | sincerity might kill you |
| |     surrounded as we are by deep tragedies |
| |     triumphs in close proximity |
| Author | we ask her how she is this morning |
| | what she has on her agenda today |
| | how she feels about her husband |
| | partner  child-minder  son  job  car |
| Narrator | irony is the perfect defence |
| Poet | unconscious irony moves deeper |
| | embedding a subtle cruelty |
| |     to break apart |
| | then irony takes up cynicism |
| | though they look askance at each other |
| |     they're bedfellows |
| Witness | cynicism thinks itself the best |
| | tut tut sit silent or laugh it off |
| |     'there are x numbers of car break ins and rising' |
| |     'mental patient released – serious threat to women |
| |       – avoid' |
| |     'oh yes we're all a bit mad round here!' |
| |     'my manager's mad |
| |       I wouldn't go home with him on the tube!' |
| Narrator | all evaporates into quips  throwaway remarks |
| | there is no deeper reality to the debate |
| Unknown Friend | well are we allowed to debate the arena of experts? |
| | surely like plunging our hands willingly into liquid ice |
| | we lay ourselves open to allegations as the chattering class |
| | bring us our serious representatives educated pundits |
| | who have years of experience bring us our mediators |
| | representatives who put forward our demands negotiate |

|  |  |
|---|---|
|  | take these people away  give us empty hands and hollow words |
|  | take away our pride in education rationality |
|  | then we can make jokes about anything |
|  |     'what she get herself go and get killed for – |
|  | fruitcake' |
|  |     what a gem abusive irony is |
| Poet | everything can have its exclamation mark! |
|  | and then counter sincerity with sentiment |
| Witness | 'she is such a sweet looking young thing |
|  |   she didn't deserve that' |
|  | 'that was such a brave thing to do |
|  | but he shouldn't have had a go' |
|  |     we have great need for fences – |
|  |     I only follow the regional news |
| Narrator | what about peaks of emotion celebration or tragedy |
|  | 'I passed!  I passed! |
|  | when I passed my driving test |
|  | – my Nan paid for my lessons – |
|  | I bought her flowers |
| Memory | we hear stories of rescue, stories told with voices that break |
|  | 'my husband has cancer' |
|  |   the tears came to my eyes and I fell silent |
|  |     except she rang up in a panic |
|  | 'it's his last Christmas we must get together |
|  | 'It won't be his last just do what we always do' |
| Poet | is this dramatic irony or irony inside out |
| Witness |   'my brother was murdered in Kentish Town' |
| Memory |   'when I was burgled at knife point |
|  |   I shook all next day with fear' |
|  | 'I was nearly raped in my bedroom |
|  |     by two intruders on New Years Eve' |
|  | and I never found out 'til she told me months later |
| Poet | irony outside in |
| Narrator | irony is bravado |
|  |   the fundamental rule of disengagement |
|  |   an advocate for employers at your |
|  |     redundancy hearing |
|  | without the high seriousness |
|  |   the young innocence |
|  |   the searching for greater people |
|  |   causes  enlightenment  future jobs |

|  |  |
|---|---|
|  | how would we ever find anything out about anyone |
|  | that even the moments of terror or reward |
|  | are the same for all of us |
| Author | 'I can't cope with all this drama |
|  | I want to stick to a routine |
|  | just give me the soaps for the tension and aggro' |
| Narrator | waiting in the pitch black tunnel |
|  | just outside Camden Town |
|  | 40 minutes in stifling heat and lack of air |
|  | person under the train |
|  | we never wake up saying we know |
|  | well I'll allow 20 minutes extra |
|  | for getting to work this morning |
|  | we never want to be part of these things |
|  | we are called upon to think about them respond |
|  | help out change our own lifestyles |
|  | we are very hard |
|  | and are glad that it wasn't us that it happened to |
| Poet | to my friend who died of AIDS |
| Witness | do I blame him? |
|  | leave him alone? |
|  | no he moved on |
|  | to a world of different friends |
|  | experts and doctors |
|  | became so much thinner |
|  | so much less approachable |
|  | suffered so much |
|  | was despairing |
| Poet | death softly unfolded her panoply |
|  | lifting gentle breaths in time to the slow |
|  | beating of her wings  then there's nothing left |
|  | but the memory and the price he paid |
|  |  |
| Author | Any Other Business |
|  | the human condition |
|  | we have to cut back |
|  | there's been an overspend |
| Witness | we're not sure of the interpretation |
|  | it's not foretold nor is there premonition |
|  | it's known that some will live and some will die |
|  | rewarded or empty handed |

Author          we've lost our sense of wonder
do us a favour and lose yours
I get up in the morning
and my sole ambition
is not to lose all my self respect by the time I go to bed

Narrator         You will have been knocked into
shouted at jostled
achieved one or two targets
paid a bill
read emails
checked your bank balance
phoned someone you liked and
decided where you would like to go on holiday
missed the right train for work
waited 17 minutes and
got cold and stressed

Author          my diary is at once unutterably boring and samey
yet to derive meaning from specific events we must
               categorise them

Poet            throw a few pieces torn from memo pads
we are mites of dust on a windy day
     unwanted molecules in sunlight
     grit that is regularly swept up
     the dancing bolus of old hair
     threads shifting about
     forgotten by the waste bin
we are a smile returned
we have thoughts to go with all of these things
     words that describe them all
we have a pattern of life that has no tap left running
     no unplugged wastepipe
     no single front door
     no speakers corner
     no right to silence

Author          do you see yourself in all this or not?
     didn't I tell you?
you think you hold the cards
     but you don't

Witness and Unknown Friend
     fact in performance
     actor in audience

## *Morning Meeting – Report on London Cellular Meiosis*

Here is a cellular structure of a most interesting kind.
Does it bear the fingerprint of reproduction within its scaffolding?
There are sections that in many ways exist without recourse to other cells.
There are routes and pathways that are all embedded and have been
    extensively mapped.
Information is carried along these pathways.
The process of division is uneven almost uncertain.
There is a great deal of apparent nervous activity along these routes.
This peaks two or three times a day.
You will notice that the edges are not clear cut and that the cellular structure
    is such that growth can take place from any one of its peripheral
    nodules.
Here in another area we find cells that behave in similar ways but the source
    of their capacity to survive and reproduce is barely dependent on the
    central cells.
There is a looped channel that flows through the central portion but it serves
    more to divide sections than to provide communication.
It has not progressed beyond the stage of a long single thread.
Now we demonstrate through further magnification that some structures
    are larger and more turgid than others.
There are degrees of turgidity.
Here – I use the arrow as indicator – we can see a large many-spiked structure
    centrally placed alongside the central channel.
This seems to be one of the vital cells within the whole as there is a great
    deal of molecular activity in and out of it and we note that much of
    this goes no further than the specific cells that are nearby.
Overall this is a massive single organism.
We define it as such because of the unity it exhibits as to texture and constant
    existence.
With the arrow I indicate an area west and north west of the centre where
    there is a peak which has a permanent spike of tissue attached to it.
This is one of the highest points and has led to speculation that some kind
    of communication system has been attempted.
We have noted a significant change in structure just south of this.
The cells here are throwing up a large, hooped webbing.
As this is recent we have examined its development closely.
On the 15th January we were authorised to take a sample
At a crucial stage of the experiment the tissue sample slipped and fell back

into the neighbouring cells and was enveloped.

Is this organism under threat from the surrounding areas or does it indeed threaten these areas?

The surrounding areas are very flaccid.

There is very little activity in these areas that is apparent to us even though we have studied it closely.

There are regular forays into these areas from the massive organism and the more vital dense tissue takes over.

These movements take place over an extended period of time and are never reversed.

The zone of zoom in the north west demonstrates an area where this has recently happened.

This particular area had only one or two very small areas of activity but now all the intervening flaccid areas have been taken up and the turgid cells have spread outwards.

The area at the northernmost edge has channels which appear to circulate around and through a boundary structure at a particular place forming a nucleus.

As we have so far been unable to establish its function with any certainty we postulate that it is a metastasis that may not be benign.

There is never any cessation of activity.

To date we have been unable to establish how this organism receives and retains its vitality and we therefore consider it to be alien to any important function.

## *The City is Body*

*'a man in himself is a city'*
the city drains the blood from my face
raises veins on the back of my hand
hairs on the back of my neck
        skin creeping on my head
        dirt under my nails
        sweat over my skin
        promises held in my hand
        time running under through my fingers
        determination never to kneel
heart as Trafalgar Square
artery as the North Circular Road (A406)
liver as Hammersmith Charing Cross Hospital
spleen as House of Commons
feet as Hungerford Foot Bridge
arms as Old Father Thames and tributaries

## *The City as Simile*

tangible  a coat of varnish  ruler
god  giant  controller  pulse  provider
forum  talk shop  waster  never needing
endless  turn  over and over  waiting
there  in my blood  here and there  now and then
child  lost  innocent  machinator  web
rival  spider  watchful  crazy paving
inert  head  heart  limbs  spleen  liver  choler
people as  city  I know  places where
crestfallen  smiles  adjudicator
both judge and juror  just eating biscuits
shouting  argument  unheard  yes  this time
too  think it out  again  there is simply
no time  no place  no space  only all three

## *The City is Metaphor*

Didn't you look in the mirror  Iron fist!
try the demolisher's ball  prolong light
full  this is a giant wart  sweet parting
Say  the rotary existence  fountain
unfeeling  modern  hand to hand  surface
pallor  engine  constant  veined  rigour
frenzy  show  incinerator  dwellers
cry victim!  stasis!  vigour!  giant boil
veiled threat  in your face  are you hungry
unclothed  in a livid  child  dawn  constant
freshness  lives in victims  busy period
surface  robot  violence  borrowed clothes
drunk  revelation  sunset  only  cold
light  street  rock  cancer  child  know what  know what

*'"do we know of any greater evil for a state than the thing that distracts it and makes it many instead of one, or a greater good than that which binds it together and makes it one . . . the individualization of these feelings is a dissolvent . . . when the citizens do not utter in unison such words as 'mine' and 'not mine' and similarly with regard to the word "alien"'*

do we love city life
because we accept that we are the same as everyone else
and are therefore not alien?
do we hate detractors of city life
because we are forced to realise that alternatives might be valid
though alien
perhaps we are at war with the city
do we prefer to be alien or different
do we love a sense of daily struggle
because we don't have to worry  are we good enough
are considered good enough for the city
do we bring the city home with us in our bones and souls
or garner hankerings for verdure and open fields
as an silent rebellion against the good of the city
what is he going to say about me and mine not mine?
it's time

Michael has won a scholarship
he is giving a concert to celebrate and I promised to go

Why has God made this man blind and mad?
Thoughtless when lit by surfeit grace
we call all our senses ours, careless glad,
not echoed in his fallen eyeless face.
And when he plays, the notes light hearts,
clear cadences sharp mirror pride, despair,
and as his skills ring out the parts –
his chords, weals caress and hopes repair.
We neglect our gifts, forgetful scorn
prints over all we have, when grace or chance,
the Angel's burden proves perfect born:
madness, blindness, need a second glance.
We hear musician's errors, dare we mock
or do nature's faults our humility unlock?

**Impetus and Structure for Lunch**

It is a fact that
## *Metonymy has the Property of Contiguity*

when opening the door silence during
take drag hear bell only after session
come lunch time later can't often briefcase
take two of these and place in the doorway
mind the step insert this way up red light
stifle all complaints engage a hollow
ruse and room is now vacant purchased
on account but when could not follow green
tried to fill the gap but stop please wash your
hands this is not the way ceiling and floors
haven't got this far the smells of forward
wave a wad cave in craven never did
pseudo charm false intern wagging finger
white balm host of new things to see paper
work did I catch you taking speaking to
not a time in time this time time's up out
will you take hope for an alteration
in sequence remit keep time next repress
there's a thinking this is honestly now
did meetings take place in all honesty
report policy's ha-ha ha never
one two thoughts too quick his steps once fell on
later this is no easy querulous
take puts papers down listen in silence
work fault lines through soundproof glass you did not
pinning quite a few diligence tries some
face met face look between there they're over
common fire sequence brings results not for
real didn't get it altogether in
rework all efforts without nostalgia
how much more that this is the last take stuck
toll must clock all look out in the open

## *Metonymy and Emotion*

hurry take time out do you feel did you?
out of something I said here's nothing you
don't specify your loss of energy
a reference impersonality
taken some time the last thing this is not
for the last time this contiguity
slams up against in the street all did you
I know is thinking try slipping past these
ones you know there's every sense contrast
tread tread tread is this imagist loss of
taking off there's things which when parts do not
reach oh heavens this bus they're so speedy
place of seeing this person now there here
slipping is this enough for liberties
no conjunctions need not apply sorry
bank for certain then not needed now that
I know you welcome closeness of bodies
surprise under our coats exciting well
moments warm glancing warm from here take out
I accost this is rampant force by words
techniques not as far no I met you here
not me human I understand passion
shot through with shocks and issuing to tell
me one per cent know what I'm saying huh
with whom? what? is proximity enough?
rich raw rare best mixed drinks topiary
well drink coffee I love the design you
tables here there opening avenues
twenty minutes up just for the fun we
eyes the restlessness of sit down with me
amongst saying what is important clear
when do you go? how we kiss and when do
measurements open possibility –
rather inappropriate deals hand in
certainties operate cascades in hand
making it error of energy to
discuss there must be how comes it on its
warming to not what I said over head
sandwiches reflection response two way

oh its two way don't we not the naming
yes the feeling stasis I haven't time
you see opportunities distance cause
no time to lose we are contiguous
all over again would you we cannot
hear where lies between agreement pale
into happy with construction my notes
did you think this is not what I heard was
(a whisper) anacoluthon we were
deflated that day signal overload
these incarnadine opposition to
explosions of breath feet and feet and feet
I forgot we're touching hot breath you going
in and up Hi this measures adjusting
perpetuity once for here and now
warn do not make green one red opening
this one's not open who did the dreaming
drawing mmm this technician is making
statements behind my back look behind you
do the naming fast before it slips on
contiguity of obfuscation
lank buildings we echo feelings colour
dying controls the symptoms of the bricks
wander back to the office did you make
another call deal he's not there rhythm
is 'She alone is seriously there'
pack up papers lunch and phone ordained
by the inanimate throw out details
remember next who I am polite to

        Did you know this is a trap? Would you mind
        can you drop by leave it with reception?
        I mourn seriously the loss of lunch
        you know how it is do you mind if. . .
        I'll work 'til 6 to make up the lost time
        reread the map judge the walking distance
        an hour no time to eat for She alone
        the tensions mount which stop is it I don't
        remember where this corridor goes am
        I on time with same yet different tiles
        uneven concrete floors busker packed

escalators endlessly throwing and
drawing A-Z turn left – I must buy
lemons tonight – such an anonymous
brick building stone steps stainless steel railings
dirty glass doors how will you know I was
there? in turn I do not intend to meet
only deposit here is the book its
all arranged one moment please up-glance
CCTV straight at me I would like
to go no one moment please I turn to
one side seriously I alone am
seriously here and their camera
records me when he comes to collect the
book at last he deliberately stands
under the camera thinking he's my
friend I look up smile for the camera
rushing back to work running out of time
I wish I were seriously alone

## *Designed to Fade*

      over the years experiment with harmonics
      as if sounds that complement will hold the keys
      to community friendship ambition and love
      well this is as maybe but best try other things
      over the years try different kinds of loving
      as if trying out superficialities or depths
      will save us from brutal thoughts and actions
      all well and good – experiment with adjusting
      to a study of different kinds of hatred
      these go soul deep or are thoughtlessly expressed
      can you avoid the blows as they fall?
      can you?
              so you see it didn't . . .
                    well there's so many of us . . .
                        we all exist out there . . .
     the interchanges can happen in truncated
     abbreviated or partial forms – be followed
     through with solicitor's letters or he came running
     towards me shouting with a hammer in his hand
I'm not sure I have survived the fading
we can echo geological or military time
water levels rising loss of invisibles
I am quite certain squinting in the bright daylight
having seen it with my own eyes how soon the grass
grows between the cracks I have also seen with my
own eyes the shifting of huge numbers into and
out of areas with one result – we are more
and we are presented with *Focus on London*
several people have done all the sums told us
there's so much to know and to be paid for
step back from the pixels to see the whole
what would we save as. . .
        symbiosis after all these years
        some cells and limbs are rejected
        some replaced in time
                deus ex machina controls the remote
                we remain in some shape or form
                        lest this fade too

## City Crane

*How many* times we think that day's begun
on wakening, and that the first few blinks
of time, of movement give us the trigger,
meaning for all the events that will follow.

*Then, with* a stroke the mechanism strikes
out sense from habitual action, replacing
the expected with a theft, a loss, or
meeting someone we didn't expect to.

*I think* we coast along by numbing or
dumbing, hoping that by saying less
than we might, the superfluity of
experience will melt away and be resolved.

*And Thee,* to whom we owe our wages and
sins, will keep the implicit Faustian
contract and not be sent out as unwanted
refugees from our sworn community.

*Out of* hope of better things and keeping
time as talisman for progress instead
of measuring the untold, unworded
filaments we need from wanted harmonies.

*Down Wall* slams the dividing line between
more than soul and soul, worker and worker,
friend and enemy – never say you don't
come up against it every day in some way.

*And obscure* as all this sounds there are simple,
bare seconds that each of us reconcile
with that which we already understand,
take as truth, knowledge, revelation.

*O harp* a clichéd symbol for aspiration,
we might use enhancèd words to capture
that which we know we never have,
coping with crowds and dry static heat.

*Again the* span of real time and real minutes
passing, stop us dead whilst we hurry down
often used pavements, away from snapping
jaws, the bare teeth of those that use us.

*Under thy* yoke I straighten my shoulders,
I see you straighten yours – we know there
is a secret – we signed this agreement
and consider it worth the time and trouble.

*O sleepless* we stumble forward – our purposes
by day and sleepless we haunt encumbrances
by night; we wish, oh how we wish, then count
how many dawns wring out the soft heart's fount.

              *'the crime of life is not time'*
              identify the crime of life

The Sphinx
        who did not fall asleep when Diotima spoke of Love
        identifies that life is the crime
        this is so simple
    we admit the fallen state as given
            free will keeps her foot in the door
            only sometimes admit we understand
            the supremacy of fallen ways
say last night for example
      I open the wine
      compliant to their needs not minding
      when their mobile rang and rang again
      and realised I had fallen victim to others
      and their rapacious need for superficiality
and yesterday
            you borrowed £20 from me
            promising to pay it back
            I admit I knew you wouldn't
            and would rather have eaten alone
            than pay for your alien ways
and today
      I refused
      I just refused all day to yield

and demanded things done now
and first and whether it was best or not
would not admit I'm burning up
other's time by my crime of I will
      this is done by refusing to admit this specific time
      has timelessness within it – here I
           *'record a space where time has no place'*
           outside human dignity or human nobility
           we move to hellish or heavenly realms
      is this possible when involved intimately in a city?
      to what place have we come where is the sense?
I understand how in the morning
I might not be the same that evening

## *Ashes*

        Last day        day to be marked
        hope day       last day will be paid
        dread day      day of thinking again
        fruitless day   dry mouthed full of fear
  sacked by letter in the post this morning
  I have the letter in my pocket right now
  going to work sick to the stomach
      they have made me so afraid
      thrown to the lions who are prowling
      waiting for crumbs of self I leave behind
      tearing strips off me
      hunting in a pack
      no remorse or pity
I walked in through the doors
they stared and did not speak
lunchtime was time to get away
    sitting on a cold street bench I cannot eat
others took pity on me that day
    let me use a private phone in a public building
desperate for a friend for support
    not there
    but the streets are a kinder place than you today
My every move is watched
    I plan to leave early at 4
I said
'I do not expect to ever be spoken to like this again.'
I must give them a run for their money
    It's the weekend
        I may return Monday
    they cannot know
        I make out I will
but that weekend after opening hours
    I remove my possessions
    with keys that are still lawfully mine
If you are reading this do you know who you are?
    am I legally now allowed to put in the address?
    and your reason what is your reason?
    (and the reader said

     these are generalities
     *'Have you included some points of detailed focus?'*)
    name? street number? company name?
     you know I cannot
     for they followed through
    with phone calls to solicitors
    and insistence on dismissal
    they can sue me
   I will never admit to being driven nearly mad with distress
The Author drew breath as if to speak with deep emotion
and the Narrator said
    I can encode with extracts from the letters so that only a few will
    guess at the truth and preserve you from more abuse or even
    legalities further down the years.  Leave everything to second guess
    and what you do read being the lie.
Followed by the Poet
     *'And if they will reply,*
     *Then give them all the lie'*
    I can break it all into anacoluthons, ride in on metonyms, elaborate
    with metaphors, state half the truth, use a prosodic term or two,
    or relate artfully, induce fear and pity.
Author
    this is it seems the only legitimate way
    they gratify themselves with high emotion
    but I may not
Narrator  there is no meeting point
      except in Bristol I saw them –
    still confident
     still bullying after all these years
    still talking, washing, working, eating, performing ritual
              illegalities
    no I didn't mean it
     don't think for a moment I was being autobiographical

## *Annual Lunch*

I walked through the park
wrapped up against a bitter wind
and drank hot chocolate at the cafe
I didn't like the way that man
                          suddenly appeared
as I passed some bushes
I slowed down and speeded up
                          and so did he
at the bottom of the slope
there were lots of people
I stopped dead
                 and he passed me
we all meet up
at the work lunch
it's great to see you
hug hug kiss kiss
we all embrace
reach past feeling to
camaraderie of the moment
fish and chips all round
with a glass of wine
         coffee more wine
one and a half hours go by
     'are you and your boyfriend
     setting up home to start a family?'
     'oh no' she said 'I'm only having one'
     and she wrinkled her nose
         The caretaker is very fat
         he said 'I'm off now 'til tomorrow
         one of my sons is very practical
         he can do anything like me'
laughter and more laughter
seconds and thirds of cheesecake
as they were leaving the next day
not a crumb left
     the bosses' daughter
     is strong athletic and accident prone
     she wears a baseball cap

     has a loud voice and a sprained knee – oh ho
     'my boyfriend threw me onto a table' she said
        'I have schizophrenia' she told me
        in a soft charming voice
        'we're married
        I caught it here working in London
        the landlady's children made too much noise
        I heard voices but I take the pills
        and now I'm fine'
'I've got it I've got it'
the blind man jumped up
    nearly knocking his chair over
       'I've got the answer to the question'
we had already moved over to the door
    'Don't get left behind'
      moving on
      see you yeah see you
      great time great to see you
      give me a ring
           bye
             bye

**Afternoon**

## Ideogrammatical Taxonomic Urbis – A Metonymic by a Heterodiegetic

(a concrete image of the scientific classification of the city – an attributed sense by someone who is positioned outside the dialogue)

Chronotypal diageses (Utter time/space interdependence of the fictional world of events)
an epistemological metapoetic (a theory of knowledge within self analysed poetry)
or semiotic teleology (or scientific signs of the study of first causes)
girning at aporia (snarling at hiatuses of meaning)
acccidie vitiates (torpor corrupts literature)

This autotelos is eristic synecdoche (This poem as an end in itself is a controversial part of the whole only)
and in what eidos? (and in what form?)
Imbricated not tychisitic (Patterned like tiles and not hit upon by chance)
with many tropes (with many figurative forms)
prosody is catalectic: (the science of versification needs a final syllable:)
saprophytic irony by iconoclasm? (organism living on rotting irony by breaking venerated images?)

They avulse with rebarbative chthonos (They tear away with repellant subterranean)
flyting agaceries homologous congeries; (cursing irritations having the same proportion as things heaped together;)
visceral simulacrum (deep felt appearances)
otiose deracinators (sterile eradicators)
cloacal avatars or orators (sewer like gods or speechifiers)
– but not yet past nonage – (– but not yet past immaturity –)
their analeptic – with heuristics (their restorative strengthening – with self deduction)
bricolages this diapason – though aleatory (rebounds this entire harmony – though dependent on chance)

Eventually valorised hegemony (Eventually evaluated leadership)
with vatic epiphenomena (with prophetic summarising sentences)
confers protean emeritus (confers variable honourable retirement)
on dirigible solipsism (on compliant self that is the only thing that exists)

Through plangent ontology (Through breast beating study of metaphysics)
and proleptic palimpsest (and anachronistic twice written parchment)
we reveal ineluctable panopticon (we show inescapable omniscience)
dietetic peon as graminiverous tergiversation (dietary labour as grass eating
        retreat from duties)
not paean (not praise)
        (Author's note: third version:
            business lunch!
            guts like office shredder
            must impress exec.
            or will get sack
            might have to
            spend more time
            with family/
            gardening)

## City Exam

1. Dear God?
2. Travel from your sheltered accommodation to Tower Bridge – choose overground transport when you have learning difficulties
3. Open the A-Z at any page and find your friend's house
4. Adjust this quote: 'Home is where you . . .'
5. Is the Mud March for you?
6. Childhood playmates are something you've always dreamed of
7. Go back over the same route again and again
8. The funeral is in Brixton
9. Locate your birthplace describe it as
10. When you are invited to a party in Forest Hill can you get back to Colindale before 3.00 am
11. Recall the Battle of Euston (I am the poet who was there – Setting: Euston Road 12.05 am; Characters: single woman pedestrian, crowd of drunken youths, taxi driver with cab; Scenario: walk through drunken youths or take the taxi: (a) with enough money for the fare or (b) without enough money).
12. Recall the gothic horror of standing at a bus-stop outside the Bank of England at 10.35 pm on a cold November night in gusting wind and rain when there is no one there
13. Buy fresh vegetables when if you have to leave your bike for a moment it will be stolen
14. Is there city in the air?
15. What becomes of you when destination is connected to thought?
16. Gather 3 days of kind words
17. When the time comes move hastily
18. Where lies the heart?
19. Can you hear the sound of breathing?
20. Here is your mother remember her
21. What was it . . .
22. Have you taken several pills?
23. List the names of . . .
24. Give the common name for Treponema Pallidum
24a. Have you been to the euphemism clinic?
    (it has a separate door at the side)
25. Have you a category?
26. Meet me by chance in the office
27. Name the attributes of love

28. Do not want to see further than the impact on the surface
29. Now

## *A Manifesto:* OED NW1

I attend a course on the use of mirrors in literature
A reflection on memory
I refer you to my poem
'What to do when old men mention sex'
Oh Mina! Mina!
I look into the plate glass
note only the buildings behind me
see only an impersonal human face
    don't show true feelings
use an expression
    that provides anonymity
there is a fault in this mirror
some of the image is blurred
        take my soul away (roars of laughter)
        take my integrity away (snort of scorn)
        take my sincerity away (oh ye heavens)
  I put this unclear image at the back
    in the foreground
    the picture is clear but not studied closely
    I see what I want to see
I look in the mirror
turning my back to the subject
I saw her when I knew she was dead
but did not believe it
    mirror the city in the soul
    mirror the city with the body
can we accept that the mirror reflects perfectly
even a convex one?
    placing us at the centre of a diminishing world
    to see and be seen
    scrutinise and see blemishes
      look in look out
        the narrator tells the stories
        reveals *mise en abyme*
        the poet compresses
        or describes
            a glimpse of the divine
                axis

now look in this concave mirror
it reverses top to toe
move to an exact point of vision
reverse the image
    clarity is not available on demand
    you certainly did feel faint that day
    later you took drugs for almost everything
    and at the time I didn't know
        you called for help
        scared in the darkness
        when the lights went out
    I felt for you and called your name
    we stumbled out into the bright sunshine
    I recall the laughter as it became more raucous
    the eyes as they became more bright
    the other that now made more impact than the self
the focus was there for a short time
    you have to stop moving
        please stand still don't move
        look you moved

sharp focus that cuts like a knife for years afterwards
    all the way up the Whitechapel Road
        passing Cable Street
            all the way to the tube station
            where the litter
            dragging its sodden shards along gutters
            tears at my ankles and intimacies
I beg you to move the mirror
    change the focus
    not leave me pinned in the centre of a concave world
        I recognise that there's the imminent threat
            of sudden and complete reversal
that's me there
    of course you can just see me
    identification of image
    with large hand written label
    this one is exhibit 4
    1-3 are crystal clear it took years to work out
    1 the curse of the riddle
    2 the twist of fate

   3 the plunge of the knife
   5 I have walked away –
in dreams I
  take out the gender
  remove the tenses
  erase the pronouns
  position the emotions with prepositions
  change the beginning and end of the sentence
    add anacoluthons
but on waking
use a sentence which you have heard before
when we sat and had tea
which was not what you had intended
with the plans
which she saw intermittently in focus
with sentences that are anacoluthic not just
phrases
  This is clear to me now
it's a sequence of details describing
  a drama a whole afternoon
  the weather we go we are
  you see you keep going out of focus
Dear Mary
firstly let me say how soon after the train had gone
she turned to me and acknowledged the truth
that the focus has to be short lived
which is newly inserted into the schedule
that you gave me
  I've been cleaning the glass and it still doesn't come clear
Dear Mary
Pippa Strachey has spoken to Miss Watts and she is quite
straightforward and then she goes on to expound in clear
sentences – without anacoluthons – that the property is expensive
but just the thing and they have agreed to sell it to us
*'Part of our building is destroyed & the rest a good deal the worse for
bombs but the library survived & I have been spending the last month or
so in wrestling with the situation. We have been saved by the kindness
of the Oxford House Students who are giving hospitality to most of the
library's contents & allowing a pitch for Miss Douie to work in . . .'*
  recall a shop which you wasted and threw away
  anacoluthic history revealed

Dear Mary
we told you
we did not want to work with you
which changed the policy for stock control
which altered –
helped us to extend the extensive blurring of aims
    we don't need a greater focus this is alright
the bank has said we can have the money and it will pay us for a bit
        a life of anacoluthons
        I have seen the pity of it
They didn't ask me – well no I – you didn't ask me – I went to the bank – you locked the door – well it seems – signed in memory of Miss Ethel Watts
    anacoluthic personality
perhaps the end is too far from the beginning and without that anacoluthon to produce a staged hiccup in the process of thought or imitate a sequence that really does add up I have opened this book and turned the pages at random traced an anacoluthic plot and perhaps this section presents a part of the whole
now am I embedding riddles?
plate glass or mirror?

the city takes the mirrors away in silence
alone in a crowd we see without being seen
in silence amongst many we have a secret voice
obtruded upon by the man who pressed himself against me
making me get off the train one stop early
its only when I get home and close the door
stand opposite the hall mirror
    which I lately cleaned
and with friends rework the composition
did you hear what happened to Mary when she –
    focus on that bit there –
    this mirror throws out double vision
        caused by the overlaying of images
        on a poorly finished surface
I told you I was an unreliable narrator
    no good at perspective
I cannot give you reliable shades of personality
    objective assessments
I know life's blood beats in another person's heart

                and beats
                        and beats time
we know the narrator controls the mirror
      we know the author controls the narrator
          we know that life controls the author
              If I spent all my time keeping that mirror clean
                    I'd lose my job

place asterisks here
in case you read something you don't want to read
in case I write something I don't want to write
and of course in case you print something you don't want to print
This hall of mirrors is due for closure

\*   \*   \*   \*   \*   \*   \*   \*   \*   \*

**Parks**

planting in the park is symmetrical
in rococo motion six or seven
lean boys jump and twist  the ball flies into
and past the net over and bounce and pass
lithe quick curves mingle  blend in the dying
heat  a hot dusty summer evening
when dull noises settle without echo
scuffing trainers on a hard court chink thud
they don't like being looked at they stare
me out I walk fast not quite sure danger
won't steam past suddenly changing my life
the children swing drift on the roundabout
over and over round and round  winos
shift places on the broken bench shouting
one jerks up  standing  pronounces and spits
but two gesture  indicate placation
each with a bottle in their hand  I see
them there many times in the evenings
when boys play football on the open slope
relieved the heat's going and they can run
no girls play here three stand shifting downcast
whispering by link fencing uneasy
truculent glare at any glance this park
is an action park all amenities
provided for by the council except
the drinks  I pass this park going to work –
empty – on the way home – full –
                like the girls
                      I glare or go straight home

## *The Unreliable Narrator*

I spend early evening idly watching
boys playing   too hot for me   but they
are oblivious   my two gathered
others from the same street in the first days
of the holidays   there were two bicycles
ownership unknown they ride them in turn
spin wheel skid brake turn   practise front bucks
rear lifts and then they fall   sometimes tears
quickly wiped or flicked away
my son is the quickest to learn   the best
do it this way   look one hand   try a circle
I sit lazily on the park bench drunk
with heavy air and hot sun   I give
no second thoughts to volatility
motion   now two   now six   now two groups
dispute   one group huddle scatter jostle
rising laughter falling words   I look up
at faces children I do not know
my book falls from my lap upside down
too lazy to bend and pick it up
*Designed to Fade*   pages torn   it's too hot
the fight broke out without warning
closing in the boys never looked up
I had to act   stop that   stop at once
I pulled away two smaller ones
but I couldn't touch the real fighters
two boys rolled down onto the path
one of them's my son   he is the best
I wait for a moment   shall I haul him away
can I hope that he'll win anyway
shall I leave him to be bloodied
limp home initiated wearing
battle colours   chin held high and then
the scream – the same I heard at Highbury
Asian man set upon by 5 white men –
shot through me like a knife   it's my son
the boys scattered   they know much more
about basal screams than I   one boy

left on the ground crumpled upside down
I didn't even have first aid   hold him
he'll have a black eye and stitches
a cut lip or has he lost a tooth
stunned he's eight and slight   I just about
lift him onto the bench what now mobile?
home? I don't know what to do stumbling
on the paperback he'll get up come round
he's the best this city is a bastard
angel stripped bare in 5 seconds
crunched up vertebrae of time

I can multiply distance against time
this city against the years equals. . .
this city derides conclusions and
torments the ones who seek answers
this city is the equals of all the combinations
but I do not know the code

## *Elegy by Images to the Passing of Words*

We are proud of our relationship
with Time but We know best
We show more than is ever recalled
so unreliably rendered into words
and We maintain our supremacy

We tantalise you with the half forgotten
make you search for words to describe Us
think hard you know We are best
Images talk   We give you all you need
there is nothing better than Us

We fight Words that describe Us
with letters of mere contiguity
We replace order with chance
We offer the illusion of coherence
with a simple picture of a single event

look in the mirror to check your make up
you know We are the only truth
We startled you with an instant portrayal
the passing of hours days or years
mean nothing to Us

We reappear unnamed undefined
unasked for refugees from the past
We too used Time once to good effect
note how the story goes without sequence
We see it through We are start and finish

We know the sphinx is in your mind's eye
with no words to describe the location
We thank you reader for giving us your Time
which once gone will leave you with just Us
We images do not accept responsibility

# Going Home/Kinetics

*'his soul has gone into the stones of the building'*
the cries of the mortally wounded rise from the tarmac
the voices of the beaten women
the children pushed out of doors and shouted at
the discreet modulated tones of the insistent lawyer
the sneering persistent voice of the journalist
the frightening shout of the bully
the flippant pert voice of the destroyer of effort
I touch a carved stone
        hear the sandblaster's whine
open a car door
        see the finisher's chamois wipe final flecks away
pick up my keys
        remember the locksmith who did me on a bitterly cold day
stand in front of authority with a stomach of fat
        telling me he's due for heart trouble while he shouts at me
don't bother with a catalogue of reverberating details
that bounce back and forth over the years
        they do not stay the same
        some things seem designed to fade

Kinaesthesia and gargantuan hubris:
the great beast lying almost dormant, encased
in scales of brick, stone, steel, cement, with eyes of glass.
Cartilaginous cells, lode engendered by imagination,
suffering from cancer, gaseous eruptions,
triplicate bureaucracy on gigantic scale,
engulfing the base political atmosphere,
sending chilling, shadowy air to outreaches.

Here lies a monster who cannot reach his tail, or
scratch his head, but must use his worker cells, programmed
to attack with T-cells, keep auto-community
in full working order, reproduce from stem cells.
We cannot feel the larger structure bearing down,
only look up to terrace roofs, catch a vista
truncated with railway lines behind, tread a patch
of muddied grass in search of fresh air.

We know how to set our sights at eye level, catch
sight of mannequins, think about food, remind with
a quick upward glance, is this the right station? Hi,
Auden, I envy your subterranean undertows
of high emotion and religion. Mundanity
does not exist. Urbanity means something else.
I am built of city dust and to city dust
I will return. I am shaped by the city,

carved out of soft, old cement, washed through by
run off, trodden on, unwanted, by people still
travelling. Monster production of roars and flows;
the eyes of grief, loss turn to catch the sodium
or halogen glow. We wish for, and are granted,
through the chink in the curtains, a guardian angel
between tea and bed, suspended moment of light,
in the night, worked, or slept through, by most of us.

## *Rush Hour*

The traffic stacks up
restless and uneven
turbulent before impetus
the lights are green
and driving past
there he is laid out
already cradled
for the last time
I did not see how
only what
and he's dead
with the coat
covering his head
who is waiting for him?
witnesses stand frozen
on the edge of the curb
can they escape truth
standing off stage?
They have folded arms
look utterly miserable
though excited by death
drama and close run thing
the bike lies sideways
two to three metres away
his black gloved hand
lies palm upwards
beckoning
witness the sirens
overlay of control
here comes dignity
expertise parceled up
in a certificate
quick sure movements
they split up
attend to the corpse
people watch
pushed back
guided forward

I slowly accelerate away
feel inwardly
an echo of empathy
hear the sound
of someone crying
at an unknown destination
heartbreak at a distance
the traffic is solidifying
they mostly don't know why
there will be a traffic burst
when an hour has passed
the meaningful flow
of unknown journeys
will start again
quickly forgetting
streaming past the place
where he briefly lay
caught out by a second's
error of juxtaposition

## A Wilderness Metaphor

shivering in bitter cold at Golders Green
not begging not looking and barely standing
wearily the ticket man opens the gates
to let you through without demanding your fare
I pressed through not far behind wincing as
cold air hit me after sitting in the train
hundreds are passing you by in the rush hour
return? have you a return journey to make?
I glance from head to toe – ragged hair old coat
hands in pockets no bag no tights cracked shoes
what use is pity or exclusivity
at this precise moment I have just £5
in my purse I pass her by £5 will buy
my ticket and sandwich for lunch tomorrow
I go back and give her £5 will this much
buy fish and chips and tea? she mumbled not looking
turned out into her wilderness the city
that has brought her this far and spewed her out
my wilderness is kept at bay home-made lunch
no newspaper this week shrug at time this time
I have trodden streets feet dragging with tiredness
after work sunsets flash amber thankfully
eaten cooked meals prepared next day's clothes
even so who can say we are ashen souled
multidudinous verisimilitude

## *Fractally*

recursive input rebounds
ever increasing impact
accumulations burgeon
events plus years equals
more and more of the similar
I am quite terrified
I have lost my way in a city
I thought I knew
    had adapted to
    mapped out
    where is the best place to live?
    what is the best job?
    who are my friends?
    who is my lover?

| | |
|---|---|
| I am shouting wildly | someone mentally ill is shouting near me |
| I'll get you | I am being mugged |
| I kept the keys | I locked myself out |
| just keep repeating | who kept ringing the doorbell late at night? |
| I want you dead | scooped up a dead rat on the forecourt |
| we *need* those security gates | looked out at the park from the train |
| you don't have the right | I had to stay till 7 |
| I don't have enough time for anything | took 2 hours not 40 minutes |
| received cheap photocopied official letter | |
| | anxiety made me turn up 1 hour early |
| how dare you | I treated you politely but never intimately |
| eyes on the till | my family won't speak to me |
| I just want | I had a row with you I'll have to stay in |
| free drinks | the car was kicked in by a drunk at random |
| free lunch | came home to find I'd been burgled |

    recursive antidote
    is having enough money in the bank
    turning on the heating when I feel like it
    buying a new washing machine
    visiting friends for the evening
    I am really happy in this job
    my child does well at this school
    regular things happen at regular times
    organisation pays off

                    enough food
                    enough sleep  optimism  opportunity   good health
         community operates repeatedly
                    warmth in the room and enough of it for some of us
         the city calculates powerfully
         wilderness reverses the parameters
                    wilderness seeps right to the heart and we live with it
                            send off greed with legislation
                            madness with asylums
                            disease with research
                            alienation with hard work
                                    and media led insistence on family values
                    I left the city for another and was clawed back
                    claimed as one of her own
                    these are kinetics recurring

and dramatic kinetics . . .
                    what do you think – myopic at the theatre
                    where I saw layers of money sitting
                    so easily on heads of glossy hair
                    carefully applied expensive make up
                    rows of white teeth fashionable blouses
                    tiers of smart suits clean clear complexions
         when I had rushed home from work bathed
         changed from less than half effective actions
         caring for a girl with grubby clothes and face
         her brother with no front teeth who can't write
         families with chips for dinner siblings
         with matching pallour and infected eyes
                            ill fitting clothes
                            dun dull hair
                            dirty hands
                            flat pale faces
                            shouting
                            shrieking voices
         what do you think as barrister in court
         ascendant on fortune's wheel bursting
         across my path at the theatre where
                    you paid for me to see this performance
                    with its artfully designed naked tableau
                         (the censor said they mustn't move)

                    rotating before my eyes  my head spins
                          the poverty is ricocheting
                            erupting round my feet
                                    unfed
                                  unwashed
                                  unmoneyed
                                  unappealing
           the impact of being paid to plaster wounds
           so deep that lives were harmed and shortened
                        what kind of kinetic is this?
                    can I be swept along with a shrug – oh
           be healed with a Fabian look – ah
           champagne provide an effervescent veil
                    and all because you have so much money –
                    hmm – I'll give you kinetics and tell jokes
           about the inadvisability
           of naked spectacle when the audience
           contains someone who knows intimately
           the results of thoughtless dispersal of wealth
                                  and clothing and health

alternatively kinetics . . .
           depression at Tufnell Park
           aspiration at Kentish Town (where the Dr is)
           no just take the depression to Kentish Town (where the Dr
           is)
           and the aspiration to Tufnell Park
           where the source of the depression lies (yes he lied)
           visit the Dr (who turned out to be a bit of a perv)
           dispense with the depression (some years later)
           move to Archway which was not totally advisable –
           change job
                    leave poverty of others behind
                    accept poverty myself
           change children for books
                    safe bet you'd think
           and complete first stage (pass Go)
                    freeing self from social conscience
           I paid more than a private rent
                    at the Housing Association squat
                    to redecorate the rooms

    I transferred my unsuccessful career to date
  to an unsuccessful home life – that's very funny
justifiably funny
    I expect you'd say I deserved it
kinetics fuelled by moving  rage  laughter  love
we think of walking through streets
    making progress
but memory rewinds through streets
    I went back after 10 years
    looked in through the window
    the curtains were unchanged

  perhaps it really is best
    stick to walking without looking back
    go with a camcorder and a friend
    to an apparently random selected street
    with random selected historical knowledge
    on a random selected day
      and pick up the vibes

  drop me off at
    Bromley Road Catford
    give me the map and post code
    I will tell you what and who I saw
    Catford Gyratory is a lifeline to thousands
    and has rhythms of traffic flow
      just as Hanger Lane Gyratory


kinetics throes . . .
    a night with promise of entertainment
    with just a bit more than enough money
    for the tube ticket I set off from home
    to the wrong tube station King's Cross mistake
    wilderness approaches – no A-Z for this
    no money for extras or just enough
    for a taxi find taxi not dressed
    for this please set me down before you get
    there he doesn't I drop all my money
    onto the pavement as I get out the
    doorman refuses to help wilderness

                has set in I have no money for a tip
                I am the wilderness I am now late
                and must creep in looked at and
                unwanted I am the beast of the wild
                I use my incorrect tube ticket to
                get home I may live in W5 but I know
                I have transformed into reject


last kinetics . . .
                just fill in your CV here please . . .
                *'So I began to explain it to them. And mentally*
                *I heard myself speak for seven years'*

                'I worked hard at school to achieve,
                clever at university and asked for more -
                trained and sought out needful roles -
                teaching so hard I could not sleep at nights.'
Police :          'oh'
                'Term's end I went on holiday to Italy,
                searching for more culture and knowledge;
                bought more clothes, saved for a flat,
                considered that I'd done the right things, then'
Family:          'ah'
                'please come home, your father's died,
                leave London, your job's not important,
                please keep me company, oh OK,
                change your job, live here, be reasonable, be'
Coroner:        'hm'
                'good – I was and the students were so easy,
                so dozy, so docile, placid, undemanding,
                stillness flew over their heads as they studied,
                my heart, held firmly, slowly freezing over.'
Police:          'oh'
                'I have to, I think, I remained good,
                I did as I was asked, how marvellous you are,
                I stayed, remaining cheerful and relegated
                to daughter status all over again, but all I really'
Family:          'ah'
                'wanted was to pack my belongings,
                return to my flat. I did when summer faded

|            | and September beckoned, renewed effort, |
|------------|---|

Coroner:     and September beckoned, renewed effort,
             clearly determined, I kissed my mother goodbye'
                 'hmm'
             'and returned to the disturbing noises, demanding,
             feverish, needs: I swung my briefcase onto the desk,
             shouted myself hoarse: why are you back
             Miss? What do you trouble with us for Miss?'

Police:          'ooh'
             'It was a question I could never answer,
             I wrestled with girls larger than myself,
             forcing an understanding of Lady Macbeth,
             empathy of Macduff's bitter torment at the loss'

Family:          'aah'
             'of all his children and wife at the hands
             of a tyrant: are you a tyrant Miss?
             Flickering resemblance to a part of me caught
             my breath for moments here and there, I stayed.'

Coroner:         'hmm'
             'Come round and help me Miss.
             Did you really make that mistake –
             the letters said she only stayed after school
             and there's no proof that I ever wrote to her at all'

Police:          'oohh'
             'I only discovered you were living
             with your pimp at the age of 15
             and idly coming to school when it suited
             and it was he who played the crucial role in what'

Family:          'aahh'
             'happens next: he took drugs, she took drugs,
             they got frightened I would tell, he hit her,
             often, then he came round and threatened
             to kill me: don't tell the police.'

Coroner:         'hmmm'
             'I continued not to sleep unless I had pills,
             I never told my mother: what did I not tell her
             that I had nothing to lose. I went
             to my friend's birthday party and said "I am OK"'

Police:          'oohh'
             'I drank vodka and more vodka –
             I am OK – I walked out into the night
             with my pills took several' and fell
             into the canal under the A406 –

Family:         'aahh'
                inquest due: before her wedding day
                and on this note: *'Sweete Themmes
                runne softly, till I end my Song'*

Coroner:        'hmmm'


We will avenge our daughters
     The Sphinx roars in distress at the death
Boudicca rises triumphant over The London Mart
only to be defeated on Watling Street
     (The Edgware Road to you)
we cannot discern how designs may unfold
you were loved and we join those who sing
of illogical conclusions, sustained innocence
unevenness built into the paving

Soft breathing smooths the darkness into balm,
Peace and dearest love, banish all from harm.
Quiet lines come first as rhetoric to the roar
Of battle cries that herald unready dawn,
Reverse dark fate, unwind the hours, heal heart
Cracked, pendant hammer strikes barely hard
Enough against the hate that by rankest,
Basest rape wrought innocents from innocence.

Our pounding feet wean real day from real night,
Our beating, fighting hearts wreak death to veins
Of gold, fearsome mockery of first light:
inhuman cruelty, sharp wounding blows
All forgiveness, calm from goodness, goes,
Then vengeance fought, life death-layered reigns.

We do not sing
     about ourselves
we show you
     of and with ourselves
I have not died neither did the Sphinx
she simply roared with laughter
at being asked the wrong question

# Symposium

we invite you to a Symposium
this has been organised by the readers
some effort must be made make a record
        why throw away the opportunity
        of hard won education and cash?
I have heard from many who will be coming
converging at the meeting place opposite
where Mary Wollstonecraft died in agony
        though agony is not for the weaker sex
        and my work is done is mine not alien
we have invited many well known names
there is a full agenda   a Greece and Rome
and the song of the joker will be sung
        the scientists will prove   the poets recite
        biographers recall   admin dealt with
The Sphinx will be on the door
Diotima will take the chair
Pippa will take the minutes
Miss Watts interprets the figures

        may I open the debate and suggest
            says the City that you try some blind faith
                why not just take me as I am?
        there are groans all round this is too much or
            too little says the heckler at the side
may I say something please   you have only
        to look at all the organisations
        councils services business enterprises
        to know that the city is organised
        fruitfully by those without blind faith
        but with pay packets charts with population
        movement governing possibilities
I do not need blind faith I need
work with a profit differential
that makes the travelling worthwhile
        go and be a politician
I need a job that gives me private space
        to be a poet
        well there's dead silence now

        followed by derision
        you think you're one of the chosen few!!!???
the sirens blare and echo over the roar of the traffic
through the train of thought
        my friend missed the King's Cross disaster by 20 minutes
            on her usual route home
                I remember the victim unidentified unnamed
                for years

this Symposium is a drinking party
and I think we will begin with a toast
TO US ALL
        I asked her to sit on my right
        I was so pleased to succeed in this
        I offered her all that was tempting
        I poured her wine   gave her fresh fruit
I've been thinking about
        the continuum created by cycles
                      of effort
            causes       targets
        life on and off the streets
          *'If this lady was a car she'd run you down'*
the cost is counted both then and now
            we have speakers who MUST take their turn
            q's and a's only at the end
let us start with the Sphinx – welcome -
whom we think should ask the question
'Why?'  why??
why start with the curse of the riddle
when we have already been through
the twist of fate   the plunge of the knife
and have reached exhibit 4
            and Diotima speaks


I heard about this Symposium when
I met Mary at the supermarket
'I haven't seen you for such a long time
did you go to the Symposium?'
'Two years ago?' 'Yes tell me about it
I heard contradictory rumours'
'Well I can't tell you everything  I wasn't
there myself but I heard from those who were.'

> On one thing they were all agreed
>> the hall was packed   the crowds waited
>> for just a glimpse of those arriving
>> cheers went up for the famous faces
>> many had been waiting for hours
>> had seen the food and drink arrive
> I know I shouldn't really spill the beans
> on this one I slipped in at the side door
> I said I was from the catering staff
>> but Diotima was there yes really
>> she began with a paeon to effort
>> rather than that any particular cause
>> as central motivation for action
>> equal pay for example and I quote:

'28. *The most obvious consequence of the present system is its creation of the belief it inflicts injustice on women. Whatever the grounds on which it may be justified by economic theory, it is only to be expected that differential payment combined with identical work should have this result. In practice it is inevitable that it should produce many instances of women weighted with responsibilities working for less pay alongside men with no such responsibilities, and no argument can convince them that this is just. The unequal pay through no fault of their own is a tangible grievance but a further and intangible injustice is felt to be inflicted, for the presumption is here raised of relative superiority and inferiority between the sexes.'

> 'Before I go any further down this road
> I would like to consider the implications
> of actions taken together as a whole . . .'

> my friend Mary on the catering staff
> says the discussion went on till 3.00a.m.
> and they were all so full of energy
>> talking through the night
> then they wanted sandwiches fresh coffee
>> things broke up a bit
> dawn came at gone 5 they drifted away
>> I don't know the outcome

> she told me
>> she liked the speech by the suffragist –
>> Pippa Strachey – so easy to follow
>> so clear so focused so successful –

'For a very short time after I had joined the Cttee the two secretaries Miss Paliser & Miss Sterling were seized with the idea of arranging a procession in imitation of the TU's. It was considered a wild idea, as ladies parading in the streets had never yet been seen but no one wanted to damp their ardour & the plan was approved & dates and some preliminaries fixed when both the originators were taken ill & vanished completely from the scene leaving myself & another junior Ctte member to deal with situation as best a cd.[?] I was completely inexperienced in every respect, she had some light knowledge of ctte work & had at any rate SEEN handbills which I never had. We spent hours of agony composing these & posters & so forth & I took on the special job of the outdoor work. The marshalling & getting bands arranging for carriages & so forth, & it was then that began what afterwards became my intimate acquaintance with the Metropolitan Police & my fond affection for members of the force of all ranks. The lighthearted way in which the scheme had been embarked on was shown by its having been cheerfully decided that it shd take place in the month of February at a period when we all wore skirts which folded round our feet. It poured with rain in the morning of the day but mercifully cleared up at lunch time & what came afterwards to be known as the Mud March went off successfully & was the first of my similar demonstrations held by ourselves & the militants. It became one of the duties of our Society to organise the National Union's demonstrations in London & these were finally very big & complicated affairs with special trains from all parts of the country – & on occasion special arrangements were made [?] with the Underground Rly which I was very proud of because they told me that it was quite unique & that we were the only people they wd have sufficient confidence in to do it for – the thing being a matter of timing in half minutes. The most complicated of these events was the arrival in London of the Suffrage Pilgrimages which came from the extremities of the British Isles by 8 routes holding meetings on their way. Eight public meetings were held in different parts of London on the same day & the next morning the 8 processions headed by bands entered Hyde Park by different gates & arrived simultaneously at exactly the right time at their proper platforms in the park.'

   no one knows quite
   what happened next
   we think reason was here and left already
        unnoticed what a joke
   sphinx as joker
   through day and night she
   skins you raw with her savage whys
         eyes alight
   joker as human
   scraping flesh adding salt

scalding laughter effort effort
                        preserve you!
human as sphinx
heart caught and tumbled
love tormented and returned
                    dark corners
where *is* reason?
the notes of your song
mocking sing again sing again
                    Da Capo

      Do cities need symposia?
          what?
      Do cities need love?
          what?
                well I'm not staying for this
                I thought there were going to be facts and figures
                    proofs and expositions
Mary told me
the Reclaim the Night Demonstration started at 10pm
and is too recent to be reported in full
many left the Symposium before the end
            in order to attend

## *Women Unite*
## *Reclaim The Night*
October 31ˢᵗ 1978

    stickers applied
    her shirt torn
    police violent
    pornographers
    violent

'*A total of sixteen women were arrested on charges of obstruction, threatening behaviour, assaulting police officers, bodily harm. Five women had to be treated in hospital with head and face injuries . . . The injured women and those arrested were the victims of men's defence of pornography. It isn't mere irony that a demonstration against violence against women produced even more violence against us . . .*'

    women tried
    charges stick
    two acquitted
    one guilty
    fine imposed
    criminal
    record stuck
    fear rubs off
    porn shops stay
    hearings delayed
    legal tactics
    haunt action
    repeated
    organising
    piecemeal
    protest again
    student unions
    donate help

'*The magistrate* (I do not name him even now), *assumed that the women had attacked the police, although no evidence of this was produced by the prosecution. He ruled out of order any attempt to give evidence of the severe injuries inflicted on the women, and also admitted he was 'as deaf as a post . . . Both women will appeal.*'

    we tried
    funds raised
    women fined

we were tried
tried no one
forgotten names
hidden history

# Lullaby

returning home on the tube utterly drained
I close my eyes  listen for the change in sound
the train bursts out of the tunnel suburban
blankety blank echoing through the spangled night
harbinger of home  It's so late and Mary
will want to get home  the baby will be asleep
one stop two stop three stop I summon my strength
lurch out into a sharp night stale hot air pushing
past my first steps  the platform is empty now
there are only a few of us this late hurrying
evaporating down the stairs into the streets
it's a half mile to walk shivering I set out
where are the extra reserves of strength to get home
11.00 and alarm set for 7 oh how
I long to see my daughter  shifting my grip
on a heavy bag I lean away set the balance
how long 10 minutes is and then I'm warm and with
smooth practiced hand I turn the key in the lock
and hear little Mary she's crying  in a rush
oh what is the matter I put my bags down meet
Mary in the hall 'she just won't sleep' an endless wail
of misery 'How long. . .?' 'for half an hour she settled
and then woke  I can't get her to settle again
poor little thing' 'I'll take her now  you go on home
thank you ever so much I'm sorry to be late'
(I was due back at 11)  I hand her the
baby-sitting money while she puts on her coat
'thank you' 'thank you so much' 'that's fine' 'see you soon' 'yeah'
'take care' 'goodbye' 'goodbye' I stand at the window
little Mary in my arms 'now angel what's up?'
Mary has only half the street to walk  already
she has turned into her house  I kiss a small
chubby face puling wrinkled  it is I who must
be watchful do the thinking  drink? change? it's routine
offer her juice  is she dry? offer her warmed milk
nothing suits shift position sing lullaby hmmm
move around morning mail left still unopened
move my bag to the kitchen for quick departure

tomorrow morning early  next day's business
plan ahead don't think about what happened today
not enough time no time no thinking sorting time
Mary's crying quietens but when I lay her down
her wails rise to a crescendo again and I
murmur reassurance endearments little one
what's up  sing a song softly, softly sweet Thames
I wake from work time to this real night . . .
I work from morning to this endless  well it seems
but how I long to get to bed myself  hush hush
dear child  if I show tiredness she'll never rest
salt in my wounds honeyed words for you there there
now there there  now oh dear what a to do hush now
a little more milk how she touches me my heart
how I need to sleep  I sit in the easy chair
hold her to me  I do not know whose eyes shut first
but I woke to recently disturbed silence
someone is shouting a front door slams its gone two
and the night will soon fade  she is so quiet now
I put her to bed in her cot she stirs so lightly
so unknowingly  this whole world shutting down
with an intake of breath

# Afterword

Peter Barry writes in his book, *Contemporary British Poetry and the City* (Manchester University Press 2000) that poetry is dominated by 'plenty of country-lane cred, and farm-and-meadow cred' (p4). His explicit differentiation between the city and the countryside unlocked and opened a door on my city life and the role it plays in my creative work. For background I went back to the classical Greek city-state as a source of inspiration and information on the origins of attitudes to women in city life. I have used what I found in Plato's *Republic* to provide a basis for our own development and use of city space. 'The Symposium' in the poem is developed with specific reference to Plato's *Symposium*.

The forms of many of the poems have been influenced by 'city poems' by other poets. Those whom I have quoted are mentioned in the notes; there are many others who are a background influence. I have combined their forms and some of their words and ideas with elements of autobiography, biography, history, fiction, fact and mythology. My central concern was to explore women's place on the A-Z. The poem puts forward different styles and forms so that we can test out our city voices. I discovered that we are definitely outdoors not indoors, involved not distant. We do not express ourselves merely as geography of the body or topography of the city. We are not just food for the flâneur – passive objects with no function but to entertain the leisured male.

*Designed to Fade* is a narrative poem. After the introductory poems it becomes a drama that unfolds during the space of one day – beginning in the early hours and ending at the same time the following day. The dramatic unities of time, place and character are almost honoured. The unknown reader, yourself and you who live in cities, also provide a similar unity that crosses the boundary between stage and audience. We are all in here: *Designed to Fade* explores how, in order to live and have a sense of future in the city, there seems to be a process of constantly replacing the past with now.

Mary Coghill,
February, 2006

# Biographical Notes

**Boudicca** (1$^{st}$ Century A.D.) was a queen of the Iceni tribe whose two daughters were raped by soldiers of the Roman occupation forces. She resolved to take revenge and gathered a great number of Celtic tribes to her cause. There was the added impetus that the Romans had been taxing the Celtic population very heavily. Their uprising took the Romans by surprise. The Celts triumphantly sacked St. Albans and Colchester and then the London Mart at King's Cross. Eventually the Romans regathered forces and defeated the Celts. Some reports place this battle at King's Cross itself, others outside London. Boudicca took poison rather than be captured.

**Philippa (Pippa) Strachey** (1872-1968) was a founder member of The Fawcett Library – now The Women's Library – and for many years a very active and prominent officer and member of various women's suffrage and employment organisations including The London Society for Women's Suffrage, Women's Service Bureau, Women's Employment Federation, London Society for Women's Service and The London and National Society for Women's Service.

**Plato** (427-347B.C.) was probably born in Athens and lived there until the execution of his close friend Socrates. He founded a famous school for philosophy in Athens. He wrote a large number of books. The precise order of their writing is not known. His *Republic* seems to have been written over a long period of time. The *Symposium* was written between 371-367B.C. The *Symposium* was a drinking party and banquet where the nature of love was discussed. He uses the device of a reported conversation between Socrates and Diotima to discuss the nature of love. Women were excluded from Symposia. The seating arrangements were significant with more important people being asked, by their pupils and admirers, to sit on their right. It was apparently not written until some years after it had taken place. This was for political reasons as some of the material in it was considered too critical of current politics. This explains the odd and complicated embedded structure of the narrative.

**Ethel Watts** (d.1960) was the first woman chartered accountant and a long serving treasurer and officer for various suffragist causes. These included Chairman of the Executive for the London and National Society for Women's Service (Formerly London Society for Women's Suffrage, dating from 1866) and Chairman of The Women Chartered Accountant's Society. This became affiliated to the National Council of Women.

**Mary Wollstonecraft** (1759-97), author of *A Vindication of the Rights of Woman* (1792) died after attempts to remove pieces of the placenta from her womb after childbirth. She caught puerperal fever and died some days later (C. Tomalin *The Life and Death of Mary Wollstonecraft* 1985 Penguin).

# Notes

All direct quotations in the text of the poem are in italics with quotation marks.

Page 9: The quotation is from Shelley, 'Mask of Anarchy'.

Page 11: 'All along the corridors . . .' This is a mnemonic for finding an exact location on an OS map. There are 6 digits. The first three refer to the horizontal axis grid reference and the last three to the vertical one. The exact position of a location is where these two lines intersect.

Page 12: A foundation poem (Greek: ktisis) was one written in praise of a city in classical Greece.

Page 26: The Greek Sphinx is a female figure with wings, an emblem of the mysterious power of death, slaying all those who cannot guess her riddle. She also has a connection with those who die prematurely.

Quotations are from James Thomson, 'The City of Dreadful Night'.

Page 32: This poem refers to techniques used by Leslie Scalapino in her poem 'way' (1988).

Page 33: This title refers to the poetry of Barbara Guest. In her article 'The Fifth Point of a Star: Barbara Guest' (2001) Lundquist quotes John Ashbery, who writes to Guest: 'One interesting thing about your work is that you employ the pronoun 'I' a great deal, though you never seem to be talking about yourself'.

Page 36/37: Quotations are from Plato, *Republic* Book VII, translated by Paul Shorey (Harvard University Press, 2000) and from Plato, *Republic* Book V, translated by Paul Shorey, (Harvard University Press, 1999).

Page 42: 'Facts' contains the paraphrase of a line 'plucks the unripe fruit of laughter' from *Republic* Book V.

Page 44: 'Nemesis' refers to Martha Vicinus' book, *The Industrial Muse: A Study of Nineteenth Century British Working Class Literature* (1974 pp. 252/3 and 262/3). She quotes from a contemporary report (1892) about Bessie Bellwood (1857-1896): "She uttered a curse that silenced an unruly coalheaver from the music hall audience. 'Speaking for five and three-quarter minutes . . . , she hurled at him an insult so bitter . . . so heavy with prophetic curse, that strong men drew and held their breath and women hid their faces and shivered.'"

The quotation is from Plato, *Republic* Book V.

Page 52: This is a reference to Akwagyiram, A and McNeil, R (2004), 'Worker Dies as Crane Snaps', *The Evening Standard,* 15th January 2004, p28: 'One man was crushed to death and another seriously injured today in an accident involving a crane at the site of the new Wembley Stadium'.

Page 54: The quote is from W. C. Williams, *Paterson,* in the Author's Note.

Page 56: Quoted from Plato, *Republic,* Book V.

Page 60: This refers to Lyn Hejinian in *Artifice and Indeterminacy: An Anthology of New Poetics* (Ed. Beach) 1998. 'Metonymy moves attention from thing to thing; its principle is combination rather than selection. Compared to metaphor, which depends on code, metonym preserves context, foregrounds interrelationship.'

Page 62: Quoted from W.H. Auden, 'Memorial for the City' in *Nones,* Faber and Faber, London, 1952.

Page 64: *Focus on London 2003* by D. Viridee and T. Williams, London Development Agency.

Page 65: In 'City Crane' the first two words of each stanza are taken from Crane's 'Brooklyn Bridge'.

Pages 66/67: The quotations are from W.H. Auden, 'Memorial for the City'.

Page 69: Quotations from Mills, *Writing in Action,* Routledge, 2002 and from 'The Lie' by Sir Walter Ralegh.

Page 76: This is a reference to the poem 'A Life-exam' by Robert Crawford in *Spirit Machines* (Jonathan Cape, London, 1999).

Page 78: 'Oh Mina! Mina!' refers to the imagist poet Mina Loy, who was often criticised for writing about sex in a frank and individual way. I have picked up this aspect of her work by referring to a poem that I have deliberately chosen to omit as conscious self-censorship.

Page 78: "Mise en abyme" was a term first associated with Gide who used it to describe how the author writes his novel within the text of the novel – as in his *Les Faux-monnayeurs* (The Counterfeiters). Gide also refers to a convex mirror and goes on to say that he prefers the representation of self as within a heraldic symbol rather than the image of self as a direct reflection in the mirror image.

Page 80: This quotation is an extract from a letter written by Philippa Strachey to Leonard Woolf, 14.1.1941, from the Leonard Woolf Collection, Sussex University Manuscripts Collection, Leonard Woolf Papers SxMs13, General Correspondence Part I Q3 Sn-Sz Box 60.

Page 90: This quote is from Carl Sandburg's 'Skyscraper'.

Page 95: See Allen Fisher's 'Brixton Fractals' in *Gravity* (Reality Street Editions, London, 2004), and also A Clarke et al., *The Colours of Infinity: The Beauty and Power of Fractals* (Clear Books).

Page 99: This quotation is from 'This Babylonian Confusion' pp124-6, from 'The Impact of the Cities 1925-1928', Bertolt Brecht, *Poems* Part One 1913-1928, edited and translated by J Willett and R Manheim, Eyre Methuen, London, 1976.

Page 101: The quotation 'Sweete Themmes . . .' is from Spenser's 'Prothalamion' written in 1596.

Page 104: The address where Mary Wollstonecraft died was 29, The Polygon, Somers Town, Kings Cross.

This line is followed by references to Plato's *Republic*, Book V.

Page 105: 'victim unidentified for years' is a reference to the Kings Cross Fire and Disaster took place on 18th November 1987. 'King's Cross Victim' *The Guardian*, 10th November 1989. The article suggests a name for this last unidentified victim.

Page 105: See *Spare Rib* (1980) vol 90 (January), p.13 for the photo of postcard of Fiat advertisement 'If it were a lady, it would get its bottom pinched. FIAT The beautiful 127 Palio' with graffiti by Jill Posener: 'If this lady was a car she'd run you down'.

Page 106: This quotation '28', is from Pippa Strachey, The Royal Commission on Equal Pay, HMSO 15.6.1945 p172, The Women's Library.

Page 107: These are notes quoted verbatim, by Pippa Strachey for a speech she made at a dinner given in her honour. The Women's Library 7/PHS Box 61.1-4/C1-C2 June 1951.

Page 109: 'Reclaim the Night' Demonstration Leaflet (31.10.1978) London, Published by Soho Sixteen Support Sisterhood, Location Women's Library Classmark 356.1532SOH.

Page 109: This quotation is an extract from article (1979) 'Soho Sixteen: Trials Continue', *Spare Rib* 89 (Dec) p.16.

www.ingramcontent.com/pod-product-compliance
Lightning Source LLC
Chambersburg PA
CBHW031156160426
43193CB00008B/388